Blue Grass Gospel

2 Church In The Wildwood, The
4 Daddy Sang Bass
8 Don't Ever Let Go Of My Hand
10 Everybody Will Be Happy Over There
7 Great Speckled Bird, The
12 Green Pastures
30 He Set Me Free
14 He Speaks To Me
16 I Saw The Light
18 I'd Rather Be An Old Time Christian
20 I'll Fly Away
22 I'm Just An Old Chunk Of Coal
24 Jesus Will Outshine Them All
26 Leave It In The Hands Of The Lord
28 Life's Railway To Heaven
31 Lord, I Hope This Day Is Good
34 Mama's Sugar
37 Me And Jesus
40 Oh Come Angel Band
42 Pilgrim, The
44 Put Something Back
50 Safely In The Arms Of Jesus
47 Someday This Old Road Won't Be So Long
52 That's The Man I'm Looking For
56 Thing Called Love, A
54 Turn Your Radio On
59 Unclouded Day, The
60 Wayfaring Stranger, The
61 Will The Circle Be Unbroken
62 Wings Of A Dove

A *PrimeTime* Publication

HAL•LEONARD®
CORPORATION
7777 W. BLUEMOUND RD. P.O. BOX 13819 MILWAUKEE, WI 53213

The Church In The Wildwood

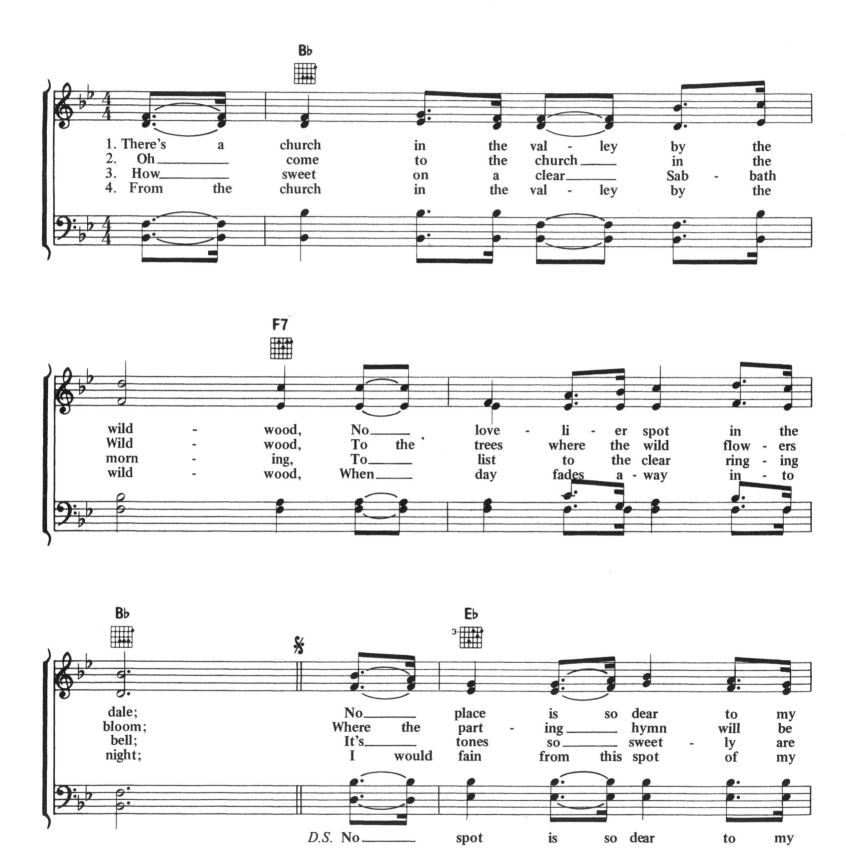

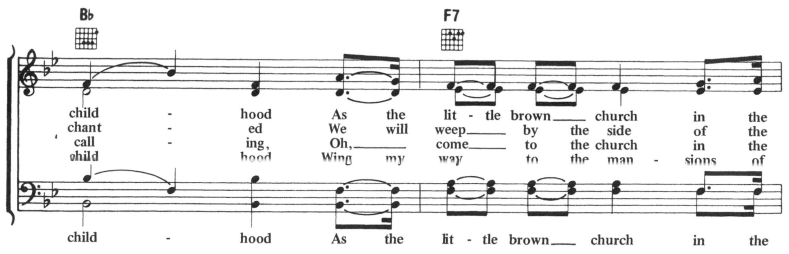

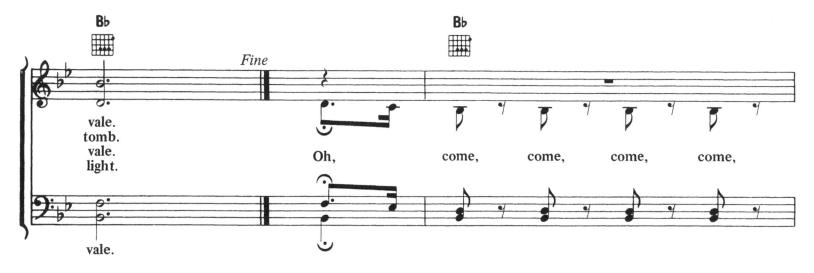

Daddy Sang Bass

By CARL PERKINS

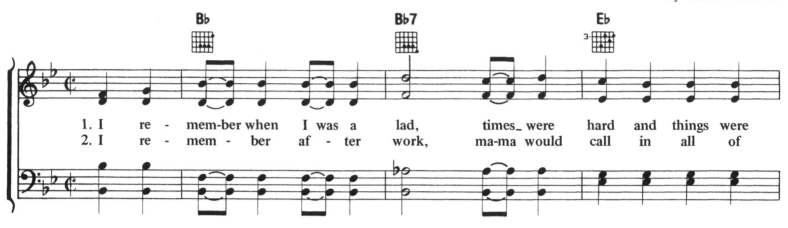

1. I re - mem-ber when I was a lad, times were hard and things were
2. I re - mem - ber af - ter work, ma-ma would call in all of

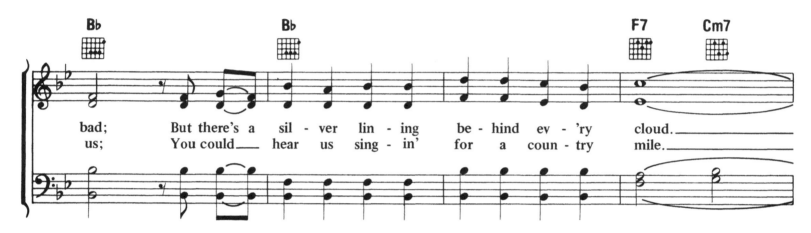

bad; But there's a sil - ver lin - ing be - hind ev - 'ry cloud.
us; You could hear us sing - in' for a coun - try mile.

Just poor peo - ple, that's all we were, try'n' to make a
Now, lit - tle broth-er has done gone on, but I'll re -

liv - in' out of black land dirt; We'd get to - geth - er in a fam - 'ly
join him in a song; We'll be to - geth - er a - gain up

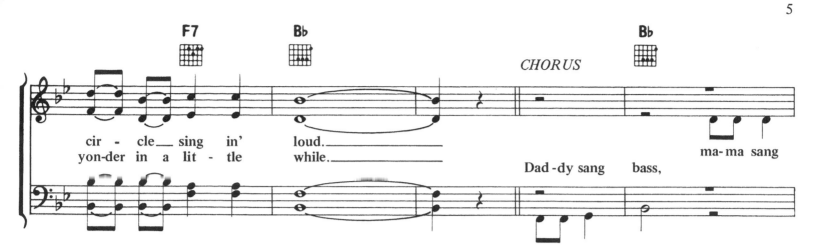

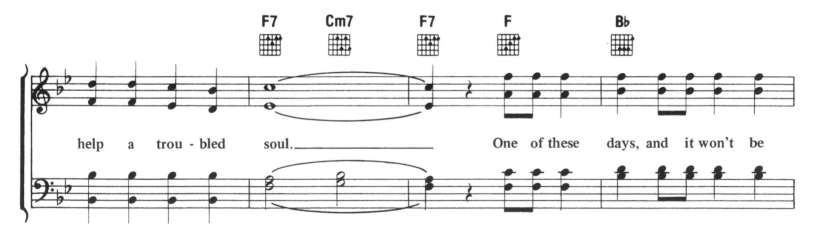

throne._____ No, the cir - cle_____ won't be bro - ken_____

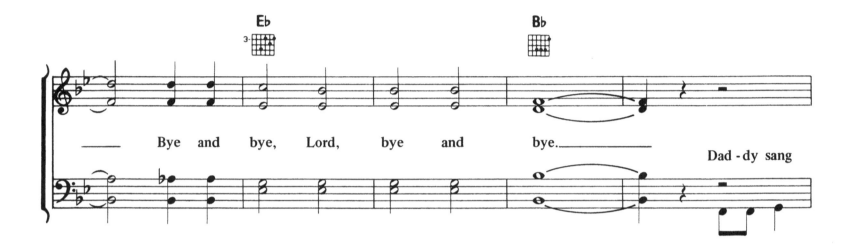

____ Bye and bye, Lord, bye and bye._____

Dad - dy sang

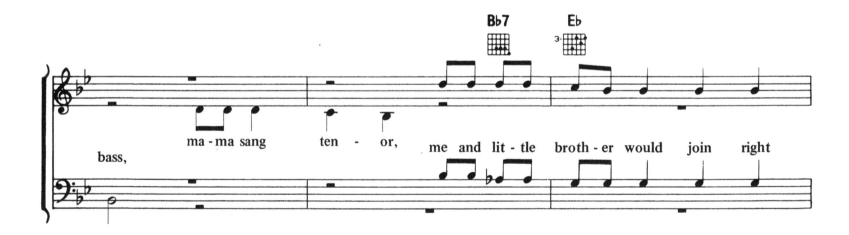

bass,   ma - ma sang   ten - or,   me and lit - tle broth - er would join right

in there, in the sky, Lord,____ in the   sky._____

The Great Speckled Bird

1. What a beau-ti-ful tho't I've been think-ing,
2. When He com-eth de-scend-ing from Heav-en,

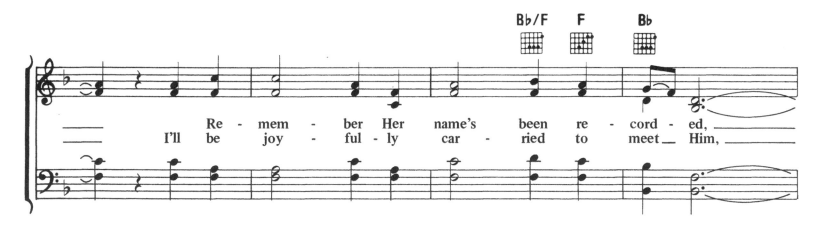

Con-cern-ing the "Great Spec-kled Bird;"
As re-cord-ed in God's Ho-ly Word;

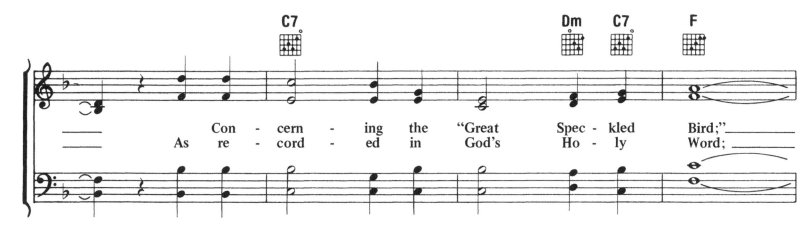

Re-mem-ber Her name's been re-cord-ed,
I'll be joy-ful-ly car-ried to meet Him,

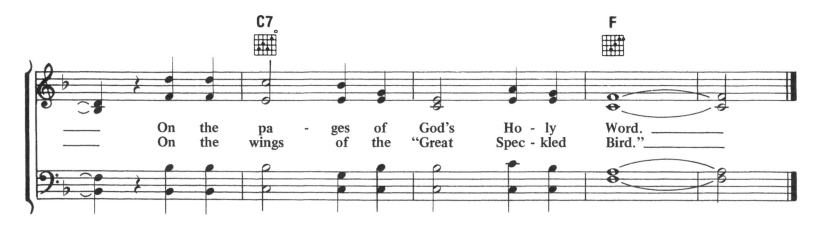

On the pa-ges of God's Ho-ly Word.
On the wings of the "Great Spec-kled Bird."

Don't Ever Let Go Of My Hand

Words & Music by
AARON BROWN & LYNDA FAYE

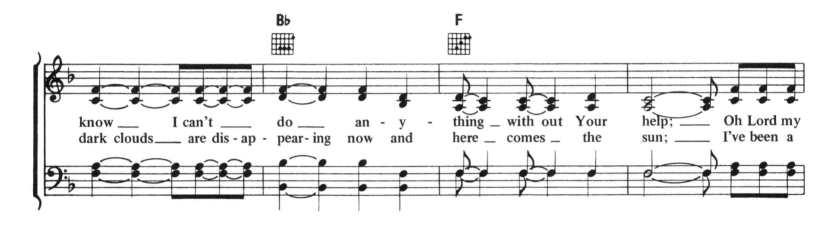

1. Lord ___ I know I ___ just can't make it by my-self, ___ And I
2. just came thru' a bat-tle Lord and thanks to You I won, ___ The

know ___ I can't ___ do ___ an-y-thing ___ with out Your help; ___ Oh Lord my
dark clouds ___ are dis-ap-pear-ing now and here ___ comes ___ the sun; ___ I've been a

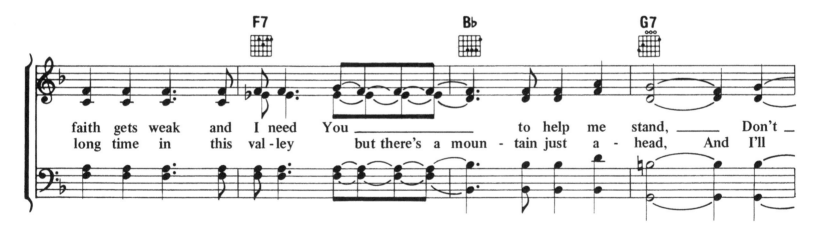

faith gets weak and I need You ___ to help me stand, ___ Don't ___
long time in this val-ley but there's a moun-tain just a-head, And I'll

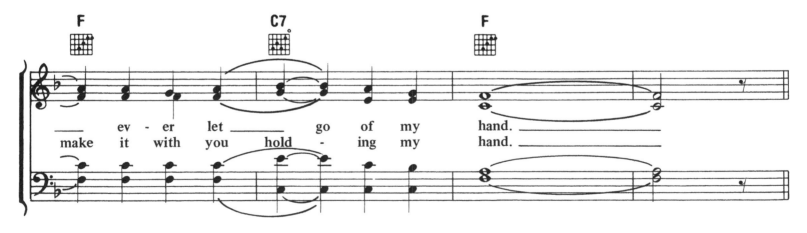

___ ev-er let ___ go of my hand. ___
make it with you hold-ing my hand. ___

When these feet of mine — grow tired from walk - ing mile ____ af -ter mile, ___ And when I

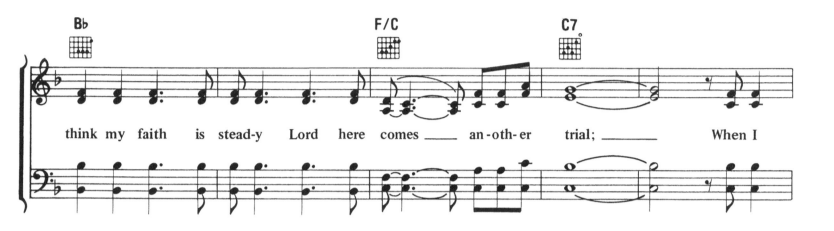

think my faith is stead-y Lord here comes ____ an -oth- er trial; ____ When I

feel the world's — a - gainst me and no - one un - der - stands, _ Don't ev - er let

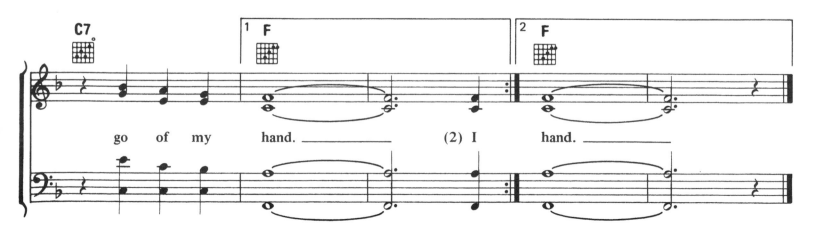

go of my hand. ____ (2) I hand. ____

Everybody Will Be Happy Over There

By E.M. BARTLETT

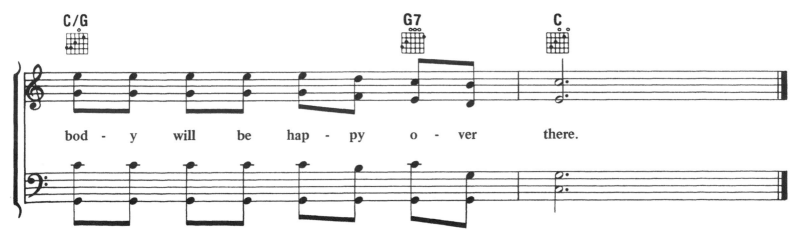

Green Pastures

By H.W. VANHOOSE

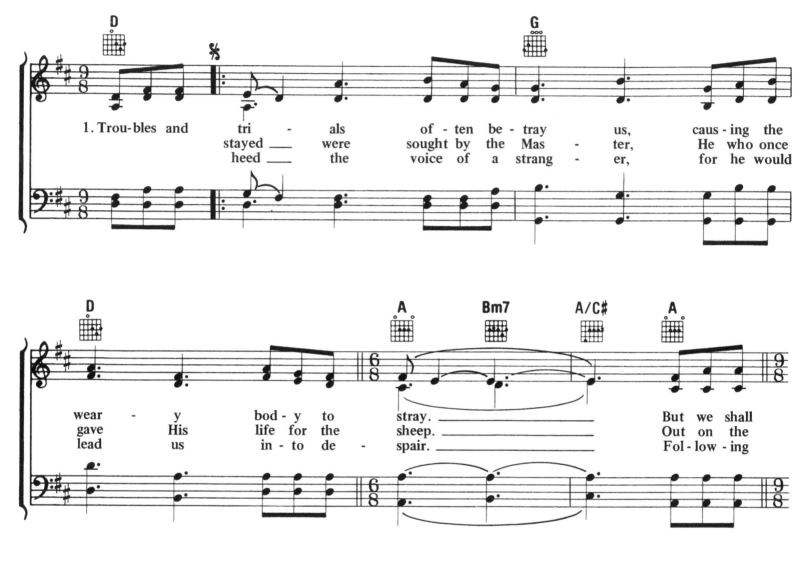

1. Trou-bles and tri - als of - ten be - tray us, caus-ing the
stayed ___ were sought by the Mas - ter, He who once
heed ___ were the voice of a strang - er, for he would

wear - y bod-y to stray. ___ But we shall
gave His life for the sheep. ___ Out on the
lead us in - to de - spair. ___ Fol - low - ing

walk ___ be - side the still wa - ter, with the Good Shep - herd lead-ing the
moun - tain still He is search - ing, bring-ing them in for - ev - er to
on ___ with Je - sus the Sav - ior, we shall all reach that coun-try so

way. _____

keep. _____

fair. _____

2.Those who have

Go - ing up

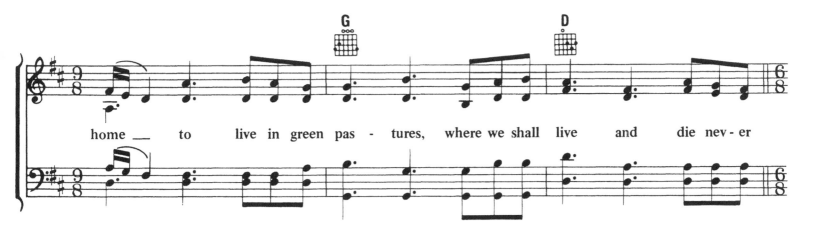

home ___ to live in green pas - tures, where we shall live and die nev - er

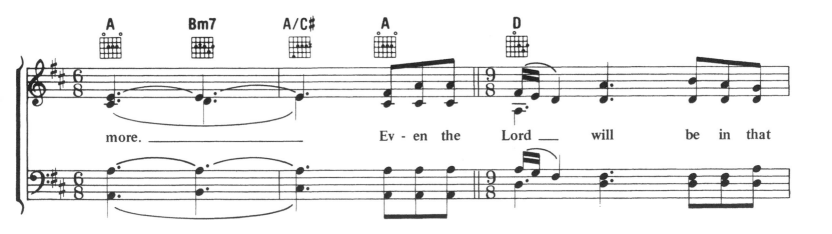

more. _____ Ev - en the Lord ___ will be in that

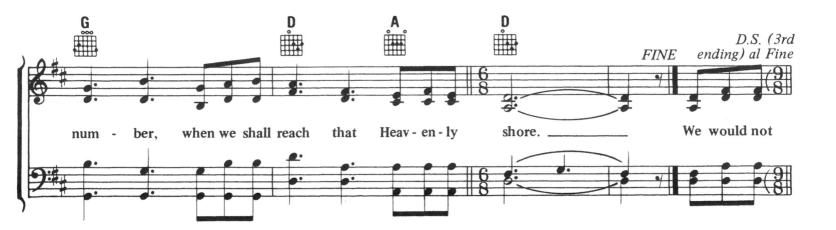

FINE *D.S. (3rd ending) al Fine*

num - ber, when we shall reach that Heav - en - ly shore. _____ We would not

He Speaks To Me

By TANYA GOODMAN

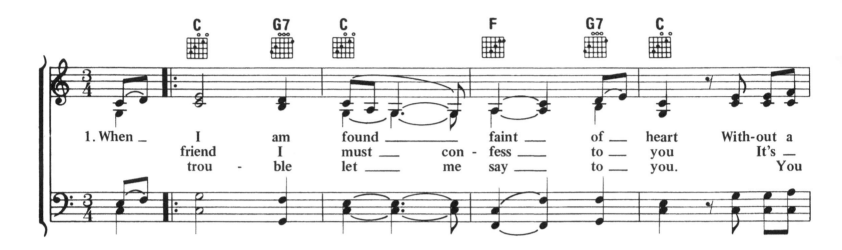

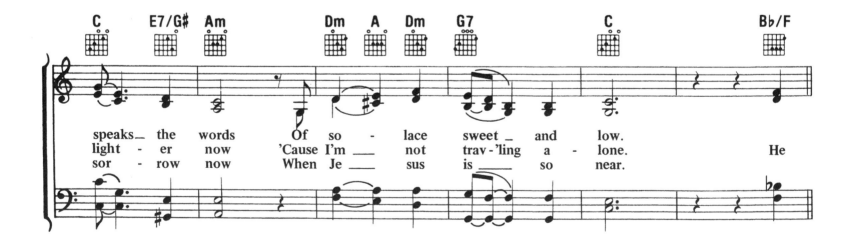

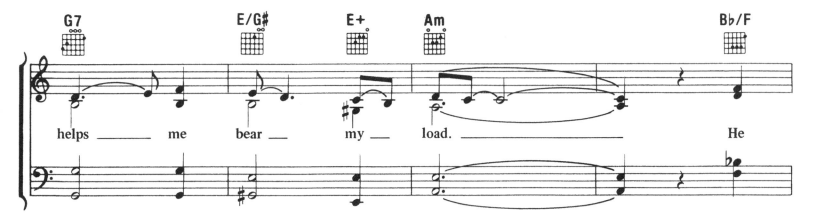

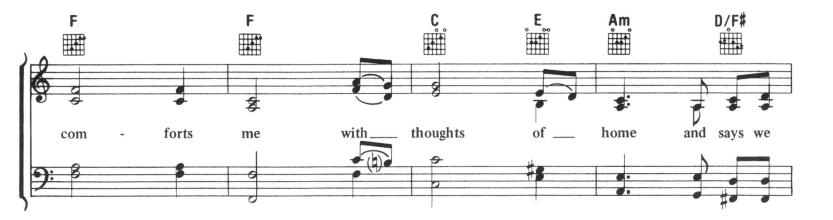

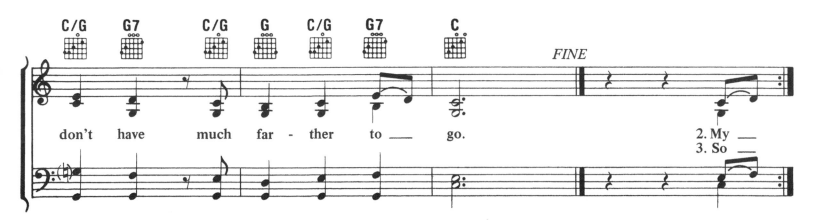

I Saw The Light

By HANK WILLIAMS

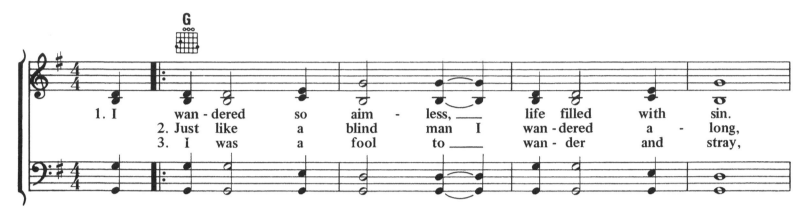

1. I wan-dered so aim-less, ___ life filled with sin.
2. Just like a blind man I wan-dered a-long,
3. I was a fool to ___ wan-der and stray,

I would-n't let my dear Sav-ior in.
Wor-ries and fears I claimed for my own.
Straight is the gate I and nar-row the way.

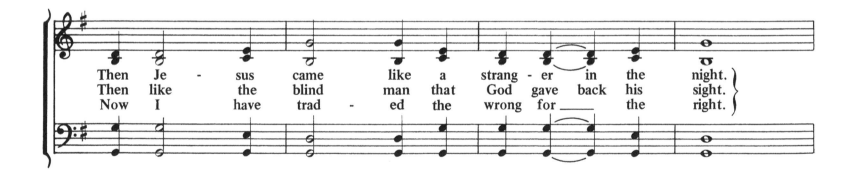

Then Je-sus came like a strang-er in the night.
Then like the blind man that God gave back his sight.
Now I have trad-ed the wrong for ___ the right.

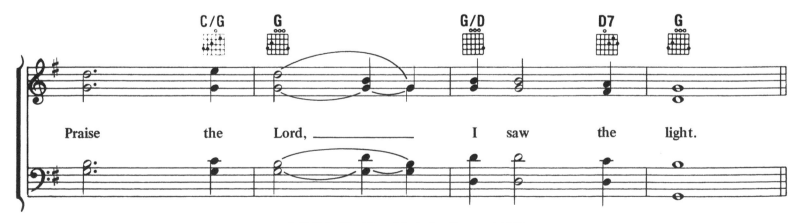

Praise the Lord, ___ I saw the light.

CHORUS

I saw the light, _____ I saw the light, _____

no more in dark - ness, no more in night. _____

Now I'm so hap - py, no sor - row in sight. _____

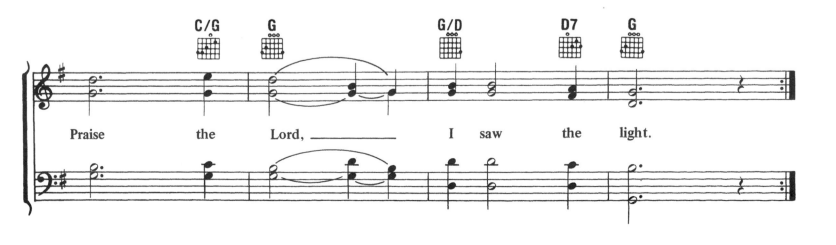

Praise the Lord, _____ I saw the light.

I'd Rather Be An Old Time Christian

By ALBERT E. BRUMLEY

CHORUS

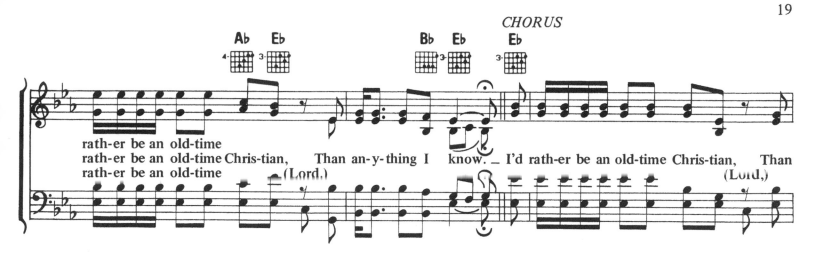

rath-er be an old-time
rath-er be an old-time Chris-tian,   Than an-y-thing I   know. _ I'd rath-er be an old-time Chris-tian,   Than
rath-er be an old-time   (Lord,)   (Lord,)

an - y - thing I   know, _____ There's   noth-ing like an old - time Chris - tian   With a

Chris - tian love to   show; _____ I'm   walk-ing in the grand old high - way,   And I'm

tell - ing ev-'ry-where I go, ___ That I'd rath - er be an old-time Chris-tian   Than an-y-thing I   know.
                                                            (Lord,)

I'll Fly Away

By ALBERT E. BRUMLEY

1. Some glad morn - ing when this life is o'er, _____
2. When the shad - ows of this life have grown, _____
3. Just a few more wea - ry days and then, _____

I'll fly a - way; _____ To a home on
fly a-way, fly a-way Like a bird from
To a land where

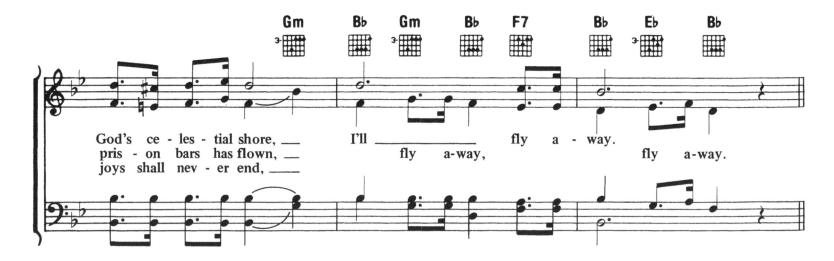

God's ce - les - tial shore, ___ I'll _____ fly a - way.
pris - on bars has flown, ___ fly a-way, fly a-way.
joys shall nev - er end, _____

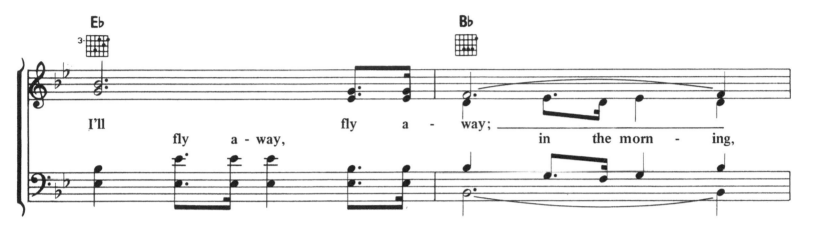

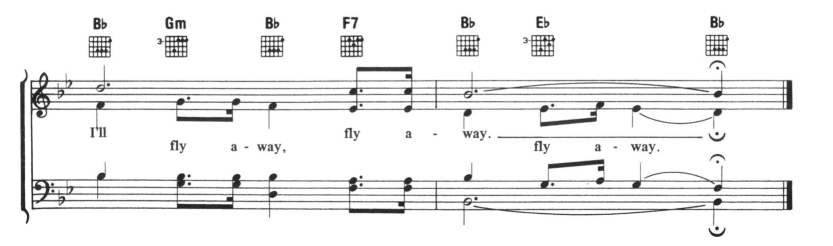

I'm Just An Old Chunk Of Coal

By BILLY JOE SHAVER

(Chorus) I'm _____ just an old chunk of coal, _____ but I'm gon-na
(Verse) I'm gon-na learn the best way to walk; _____ I'm gon-na

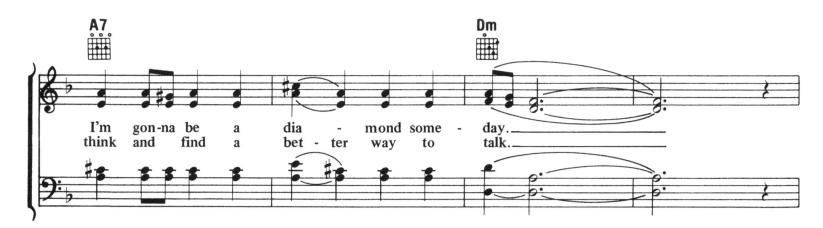

I'm gon-na be a dia - mond some - day. _____
think and find a bet - ter way to talk. _____

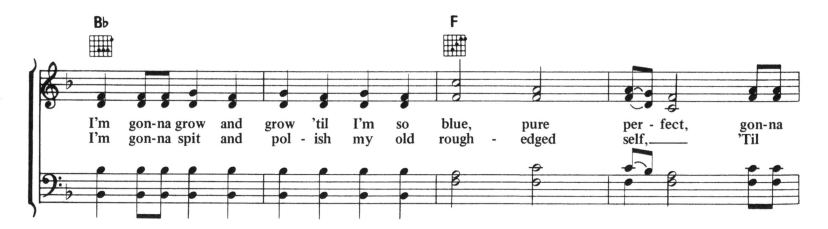

I'm gon-na grow and grow 'til I'm so blue, pure per - fect, gon-na
I'm gon-na spit and pol - ish my old rough - edged self, _____ 'Til

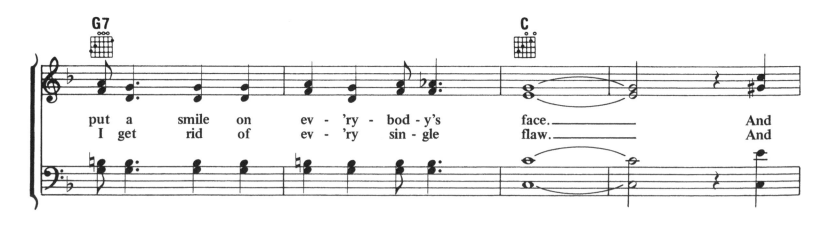

put a smile on ev - 'ry - bod - y's face. _____ And
I get rid of ev - 'ry sin - gle flaw. _____ And

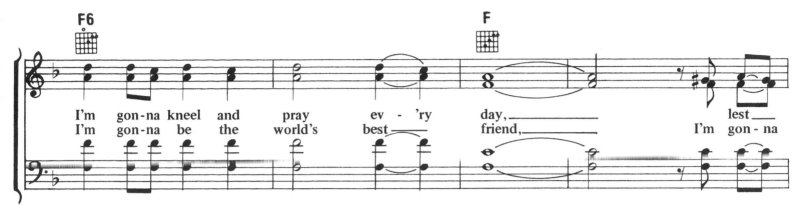

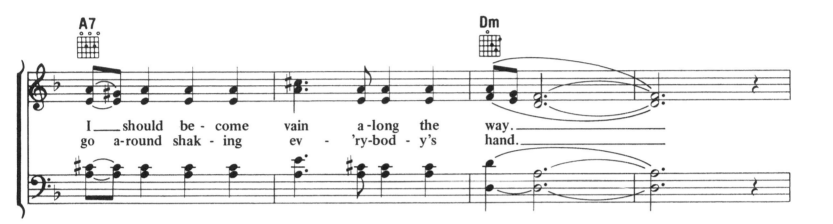

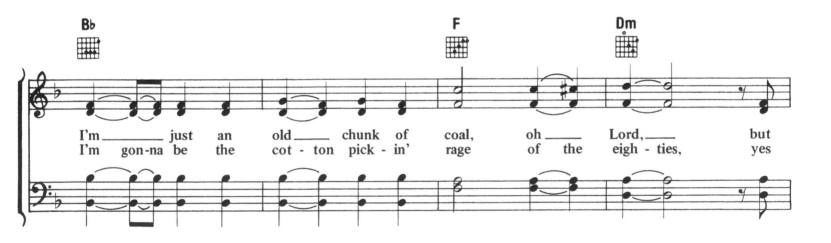

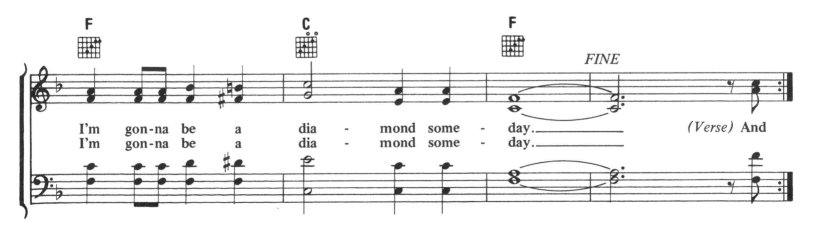

Jesus Will Outshine Them All

By GORDON JENSEN

Man - sions will glis - ten on the Hills____ of Glo - ry, Hap - py re -

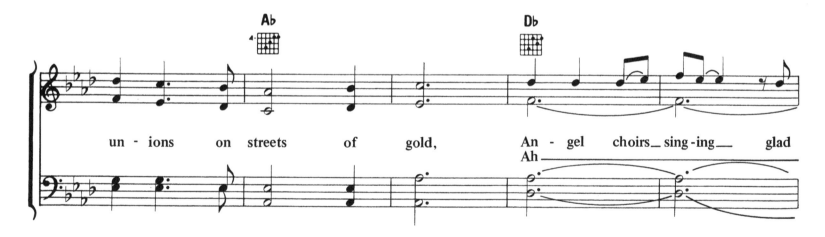

un - ions on streets of gold, An - gel choirs__ sing - ing__ glad
Ah _____

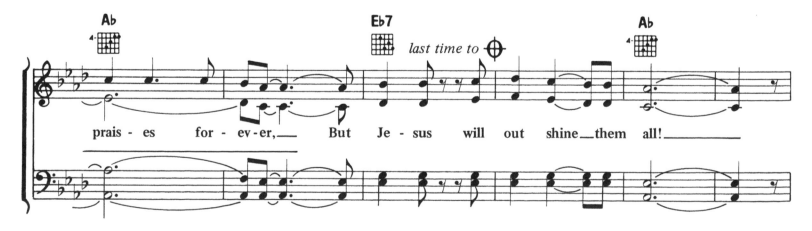

prais - es for - ev - er,___ But Je - sus will out shine__ them all!_____

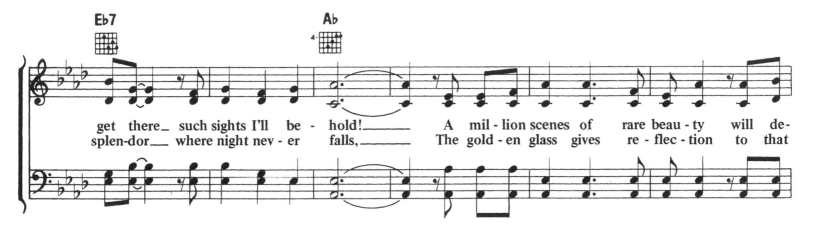

1. Oh,___ what glo-ry___ a-waits me___ in Heav-en's___ bright cit-y,___ When I
2. The spark-ling riv-er___ is flow-ing,___ Hap-py fac-es___ all glow-ing,___ Land of

get there___ such sights I'll be-hold!___ A mil-lion scenes of rare beau-ty will de-
splen-dor___ where night nev-er falls,___ The gold-en glass gives re-flec-tion to that

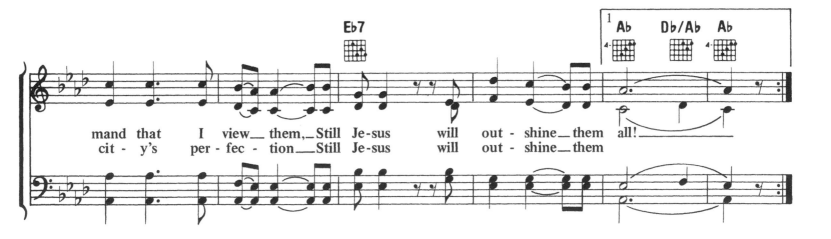

mand that I view___ them, Still Je-sus will out-shine___ them all!___
cit-y's per-fec-tion___ Still Je-sus will out-shine___ them

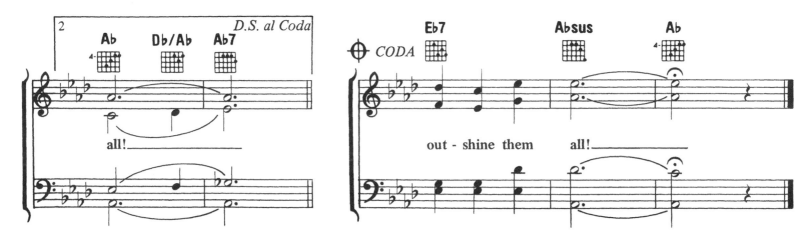

all!___

D.S. al Coda

CODA

out-shine them all!___

Leave It In The Hands Of The Lord

By DAVE LEHMAN
and JIM BLACK

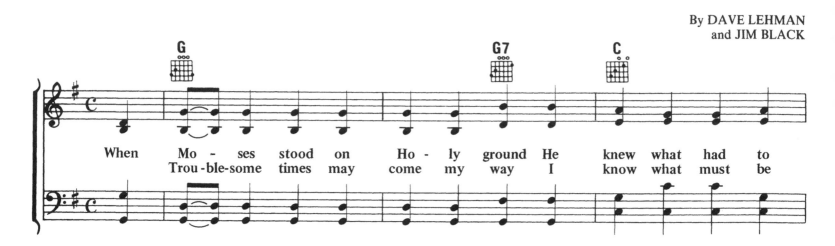

When Mo - ses stood on Ho - ly ground He knew what had to
Trou - ble - some times may come my way I know what must be

be He went straight to___ Phar - aoh said "Set my peo - ple
done point - ing those who have gone a - stray___ Safe - ly to their

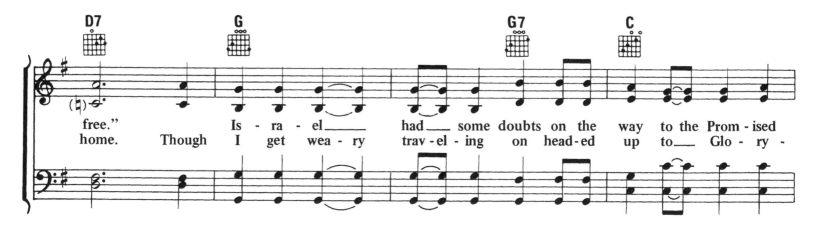

free." Though Is - ra - el___ had___ some doubts on the way to the Prom - ised
home. Though I get wea - ry trav - el - ing on head - ed up to___ Glo - ry -

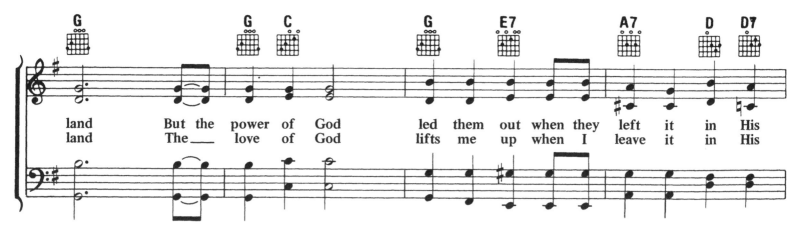

land But the power of God led them out when they left it in His
land The___ love of God lifts me up when I leave it in His

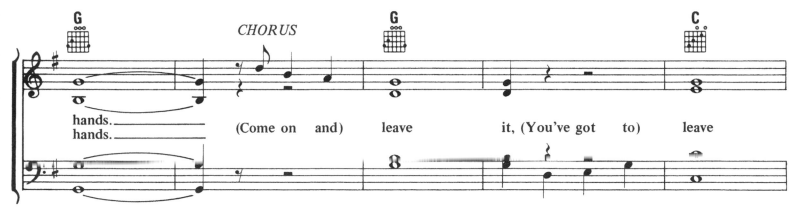

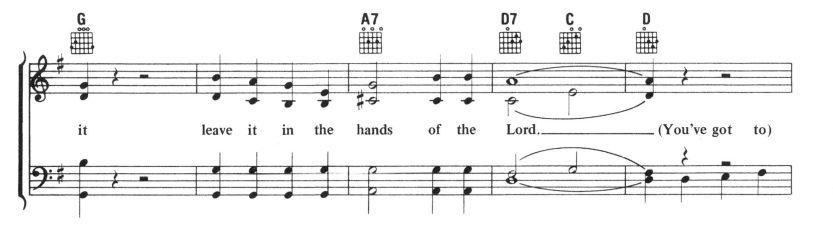

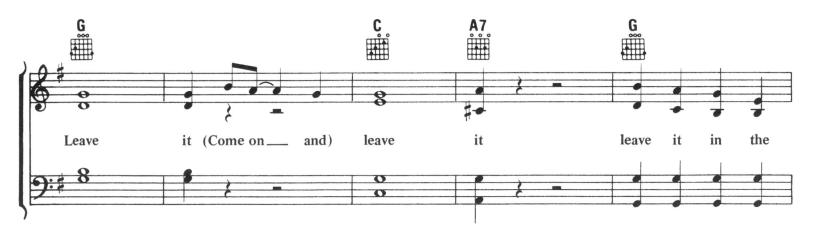

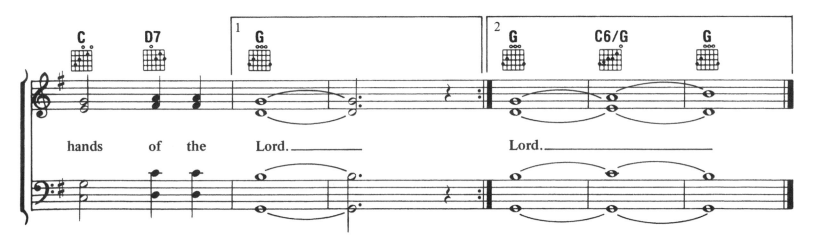

Life's Railway To Heaven

tun - nels; Never fal - ter, nev - er quail; Keep your
struc - tion, Do your du - ty, nev - er fail; Keep your
Je - sus; Nev - er fal - ter, nev - er fail; Keep your
ton - dent, God the Fa - ther, God the Son, With the

hand up - on the throt - tle, And your eye up - on the rail.
hand up - on the throt - tle, And your eye up - on the rail.
hand up - on the throt - tle, And your eye up - on the rail.
heart - y joy - ous plaud - it, "Wea - ry pil - grim, wel - come home!"

CHORUS

Bless - ed Sav - ior, Thou wilt guide us, Till we reach that bliss - ful

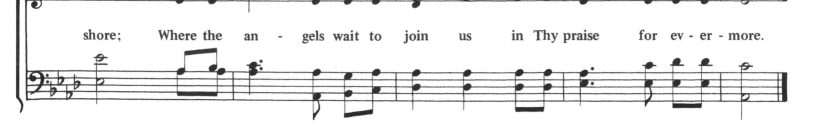

shore; Where the an - gels wait to join us in Thy praise for ev - er - more.

He Set Me Free

By ALBERT E. BRUMLEY

Lord, I Hope This Day Is Good

By DAVE HANNER

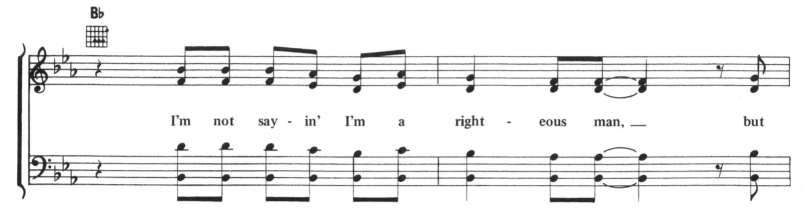

I'm not say-in' I'm a right-eous man, ___ but

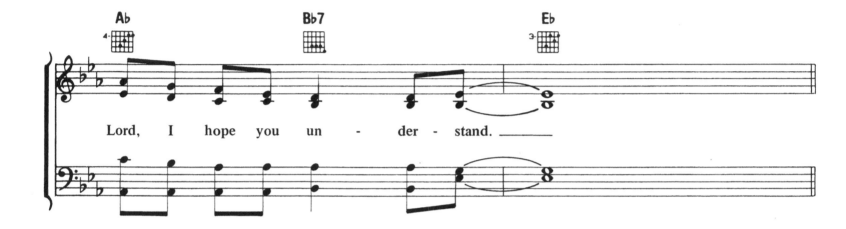

Lord, I hope you un-der-stand. ___

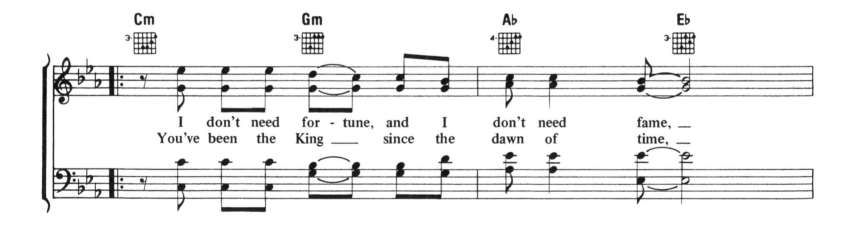

I don't need for-tune, and I don't need fame, ___
You've been the King ___ since the dawn of time, ___

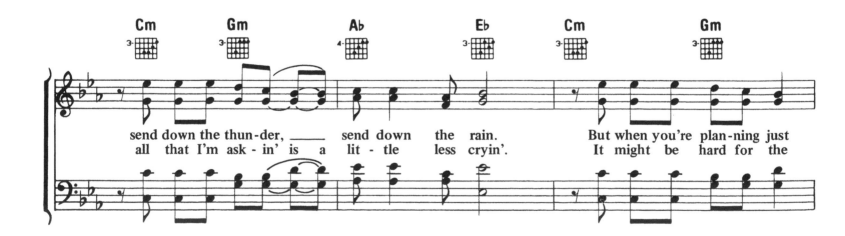

send down the thun-der, ___ send down the rain. But when you're plan-ning just
all that I'm ask-in' is a lit-tle less cryin'. It might be hard for the

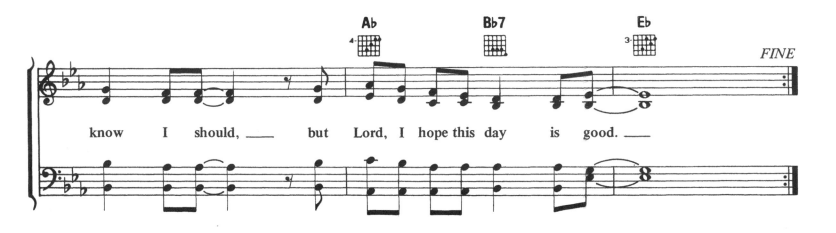

Mama's Sugar

By SONNY THROCKMORTON

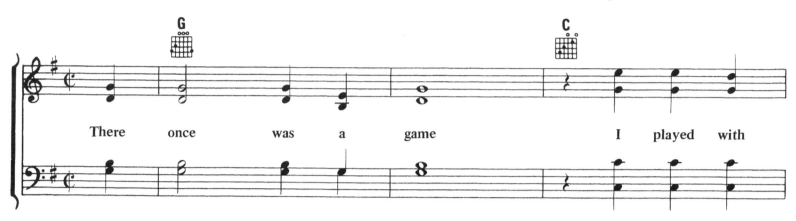

There once was a game I played with

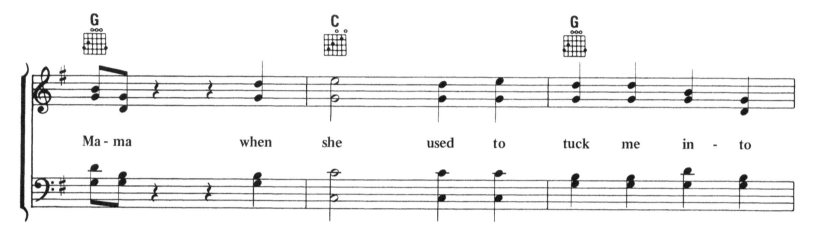

Ma - ma when she used to tuck me in - to

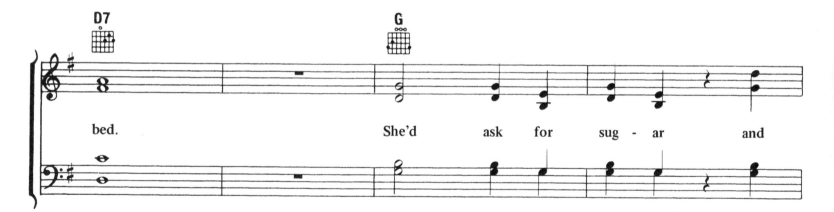

bed. She'd ask for sug - ar and

I'd nev - er give it, But she'd kiss me and

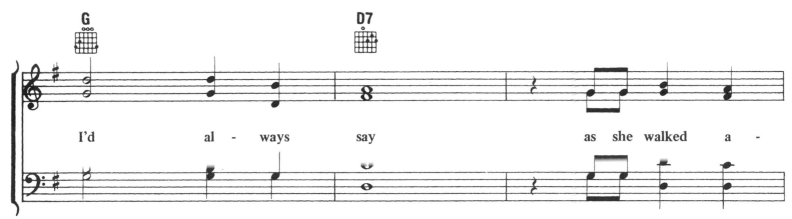

I'd al-ways say as she walked a-

CHORUS

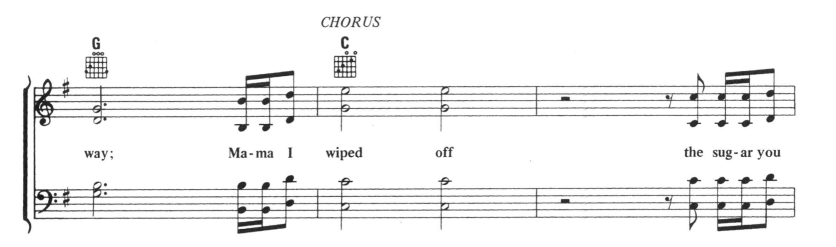

way; Ma-ma I wiped off the sug-ar you

gave me; You know it's not

there _____ an-y-more. She said, "Boy, don't you

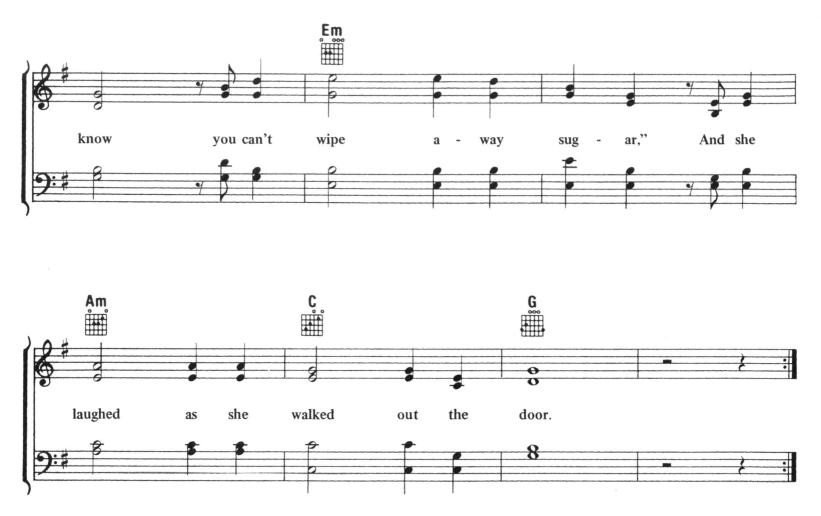

know you can't wipe a-way sug-ar," And she

laughed as she walked out the door.

2. Seems like just yesterday I came home from college,
   Feeling grown as could be.
   She welcomed me home with a kiss on the forehead,
   And I wiped it off on my sleeve, and she laughed at me.

2nd CHORUS: Mama, I wiped off the sugar you gave,
              You know it's not there anymore.
              She said, "Boy, don't you know you can't wipe away sugar,"
              And laughed like we'd always done before.

3. I remember the last time I saw my Mama,
   Just 'fore God called her away.
   There in her bed I reached down, she kissed me,
   And I choked on what I had to say, but I had to say. . .

3rd CHORUS: Mama, I wiped off the sugar you gave me,
              You know it's not there anymore.
              She winded as to say, "You can't wipe away sugar,"
              And I cried as I walked out the door.

4th CHORUS: Mama, I wiped off the sugar you gave,
              But if you can hear what I say,
              We both know it was just a game we were playing,
              And you can't wipe the sugar away.

5th CHORUS: Mama, I've still got the sugar you gave me,
              And if you can hear what I say,
              I'm glad it was just a game we were playing,
              And you can't wipe the sugar away.

Me And Jesus

By TOM T. HALL

We don't need an-y-bod-y to

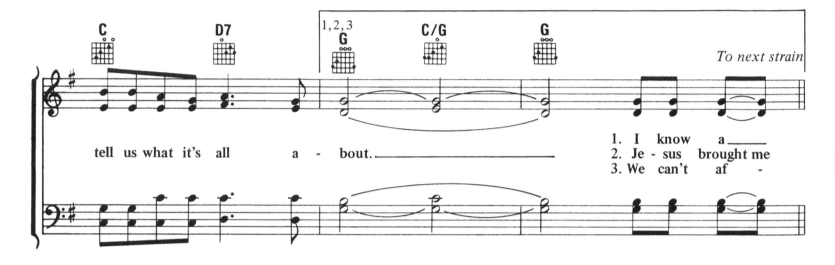

tell us what it's all a - bout._____

1. I know a_____
2. Je - sus brought me
3. We can't af -

To next strain

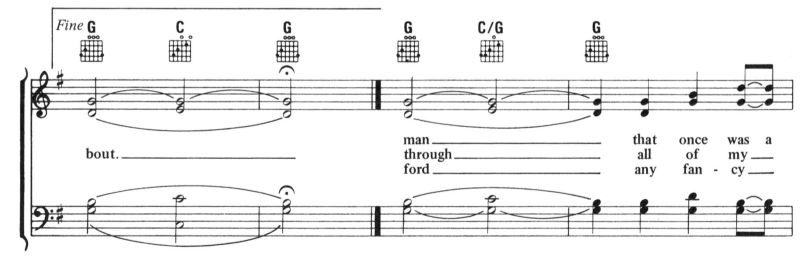

Fine

bout._____

man_____ that once was a
through_____ all of my___
ford_____ any fan-cy___

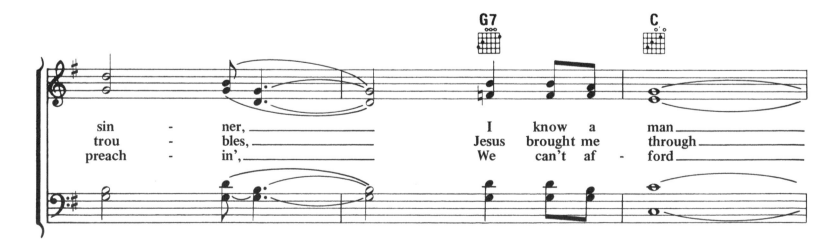

sin - ner,_____
trou - bles,_____
preach - in',_____

I know a man
Jesus brought me
We can't af - ford

through_____

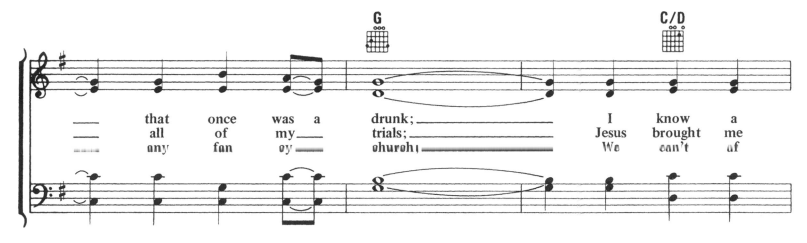

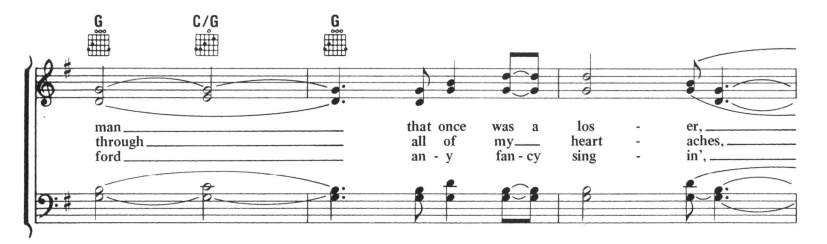

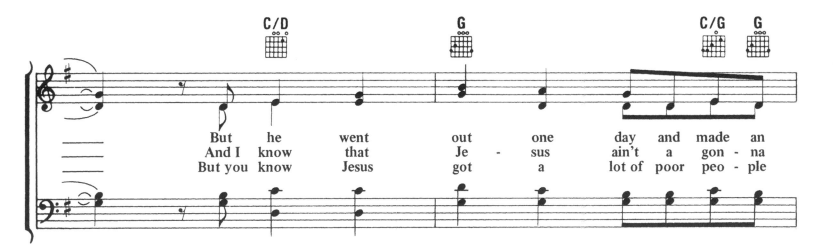

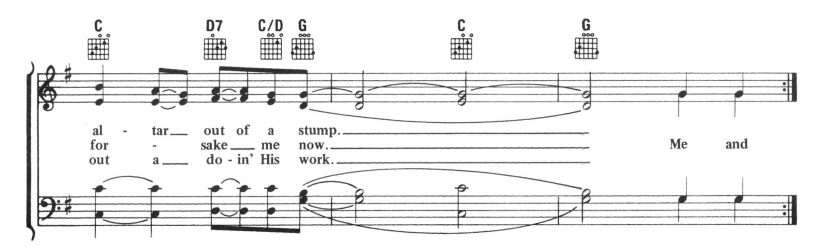

Oh Come Angel Band

1. My lat - est sun is sink - ing fast, My
2. I know I'm nearing - the ho - ly ranks Of
3. I've al - most gained my heaven - ly home, My
4. O bear my long - ing heart to Him, Who

race is near - ly run; _____ My _____ strong - est tri - als
friends and kin - dred dear, _____ For I brush the dews on
spir - it loud - ly sings; _____ Thy _____ ho - ly ones, be -
bled and died - for me; _____ Whose _____ blood now cleans - es

now are past, My tri - umph is be - gun. _____
Jor - dan's banks, The cross - ing must be near. _____
hold, they come! I hear the noise of wings. _____
from all sin, And gives me vic - to - ry. _____

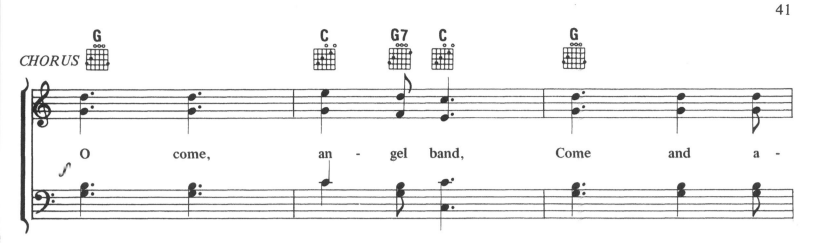

CHORUS

O come, an - gel band, Come and a -

round me stand; O bear me a - way on your snow - y wings To

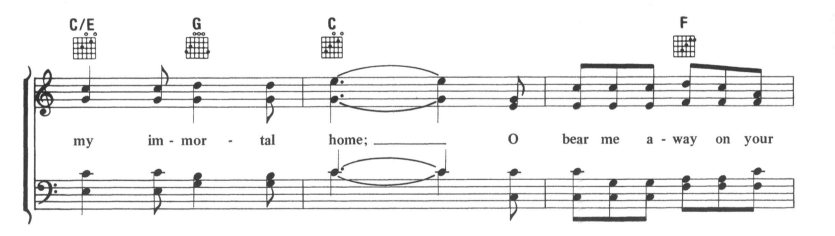

my im - mor - tal home; _____ O bear me a - way on your

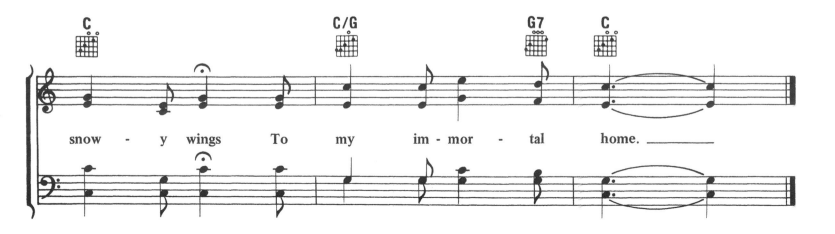

snow - y wings To my im - mor - tal home. _____

The Pilgrim

Words & Music by Honeytree

1. I am a pil - grim, but not a___ ram - bler. There is a path-
strang - er, but not an___ or - phan. There is a man-

- way meant just for me. I on - ly fum - ble when I won't
- sion pre - pared for me. I'm go - in' home___ now to meet my

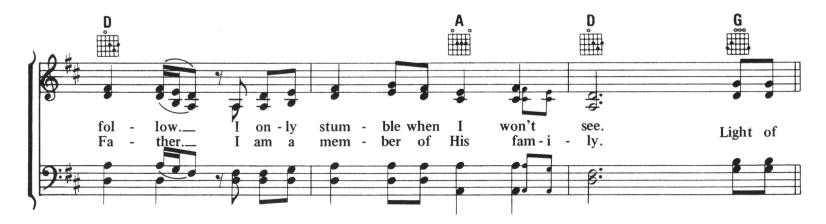

fol - low.___ I on - ly stum - ble when I won't see. Light of
Fa - ther.___ I am a mem - ber of His fam - i - ly.

CHORUS

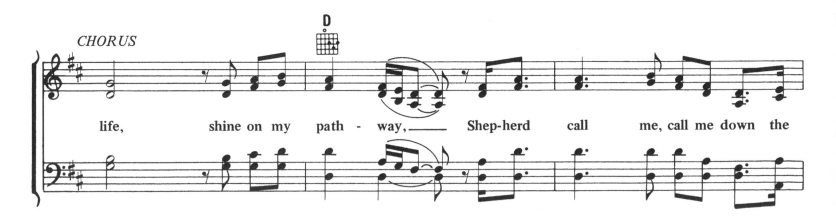

life, shine on my path - way,___ Shep - herd call me, call me down the

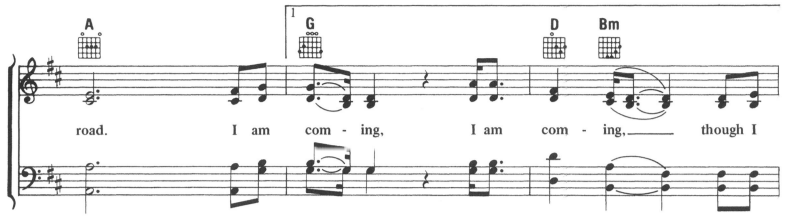

road. I am com - ing, I am com - ing,_____ though I

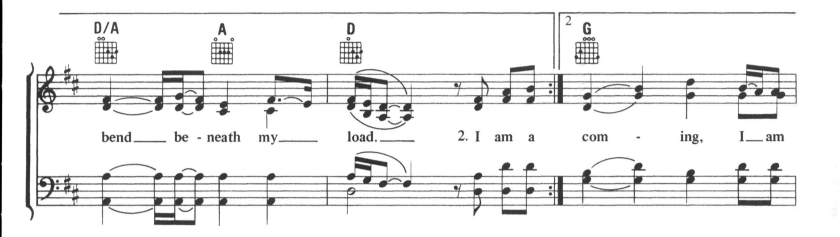

bend____ be - neath my____ load.____ 2. I am a com - ing, I am

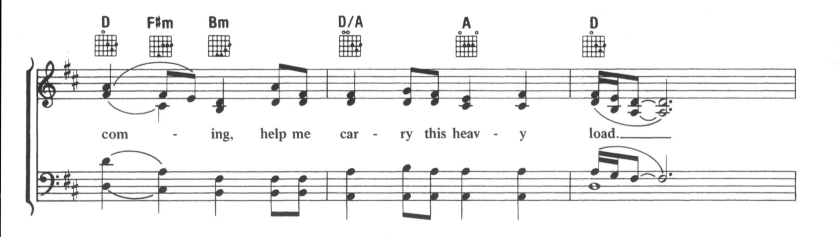

com - ing, help me car - ry this heav - y load._____

Repeat several times

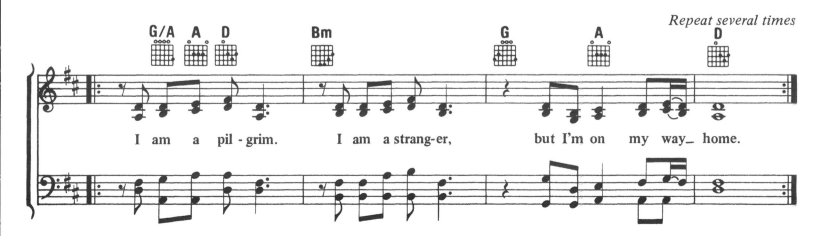

I am a pil - grim. I am a strang - er, but I'm on my way_ home.

Put Something Back

By AARON WILBURN
and JOE HUFFMAN

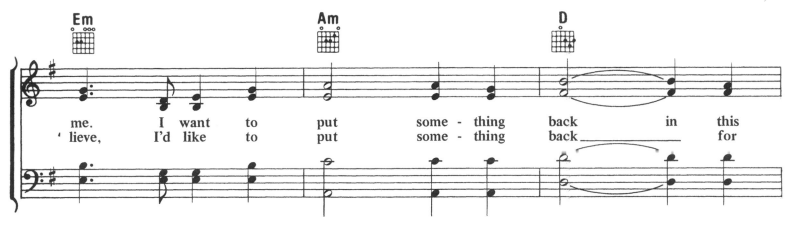

me.   I   want   to   put   some - thing   back   in   this

' lieve,   I'd   like   to   put   some - thing   back _____   for

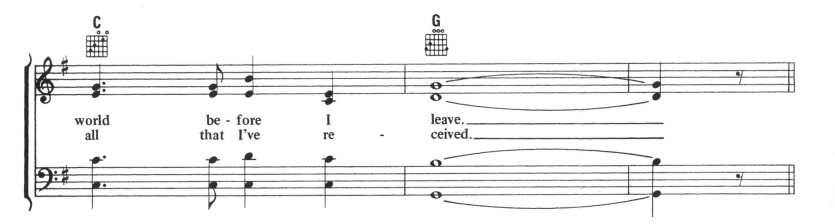

world   be - fore   I   leave. _____

all   that I've   re - ceived. _____

CHORUS

I   want   to   put   some - thing   back   in   this

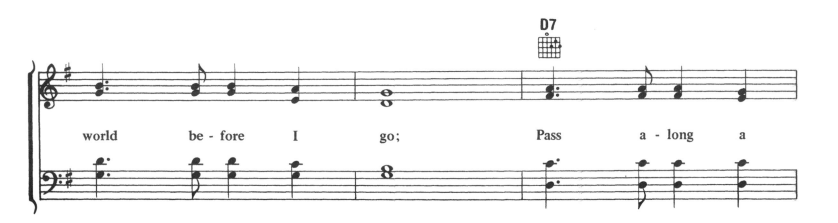

world   be - fore   I   go;   Pass   a - long   a

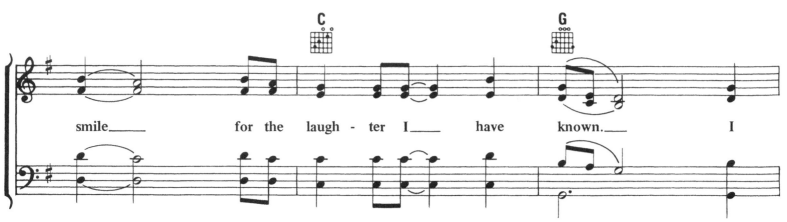

smile_____ for the laugh - ter I____ have known.____ I

love the life I'm liv - ing,_____ I need to show it by___ my

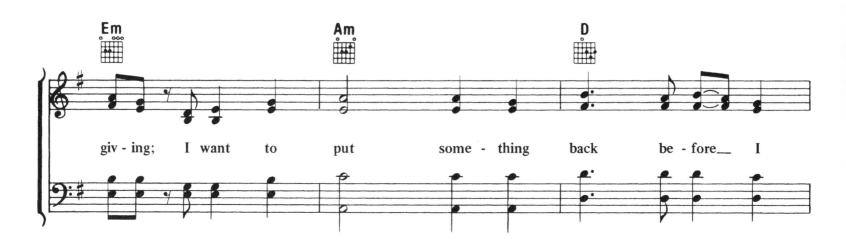

giv - ing; I want to put some - thing back be - fore__ I

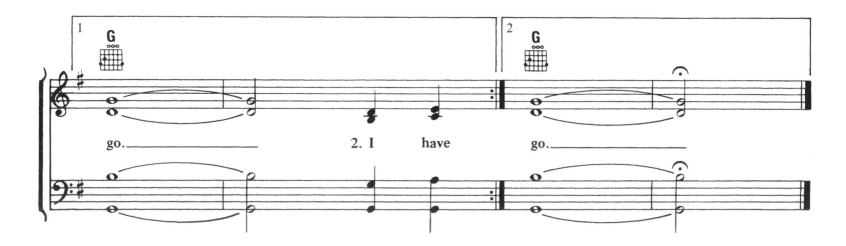

go._____ 2. I have go._____

Someday This Old Road Won't Be So Long

By BUDDY CANNON &
RALEIGH SQUIRES

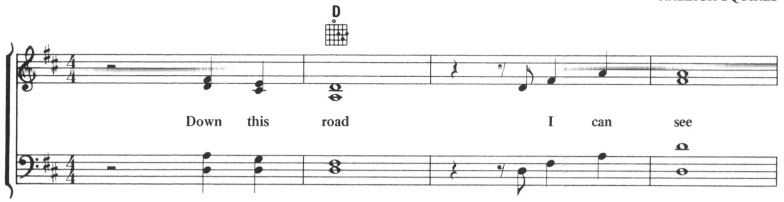

Down this road   I can see

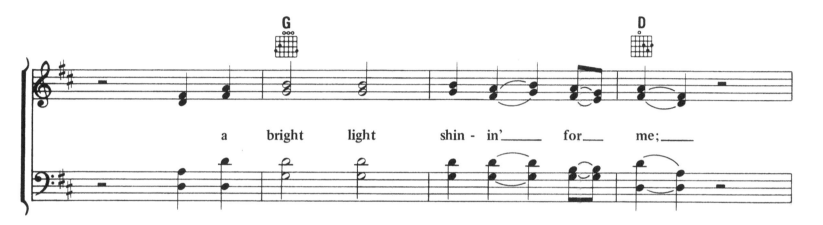

a bright light   shin - in'_____ for___ me;___

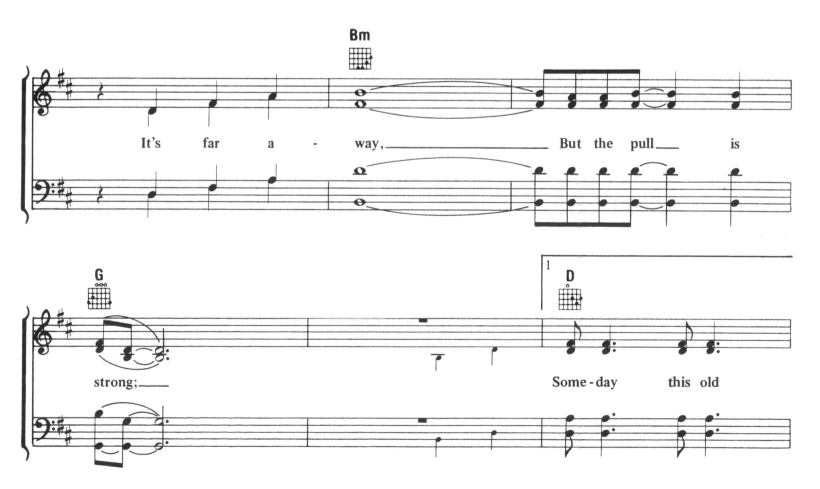

It's far a - way,_____ But the pull___ is

strong;_____   Some - day   this old

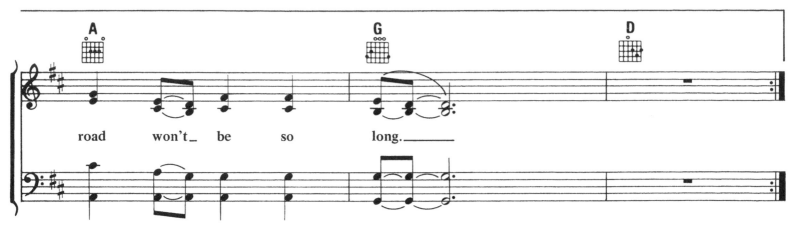

road won't__ be so long._____

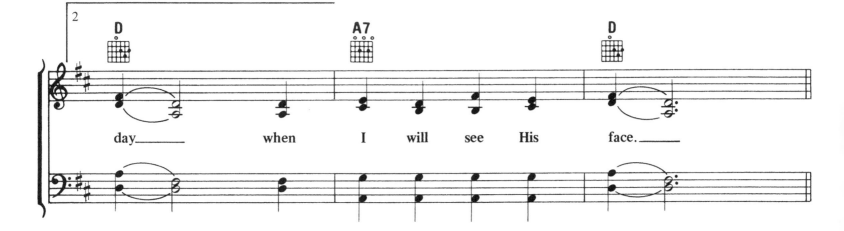

day_____ when I will see His face._____

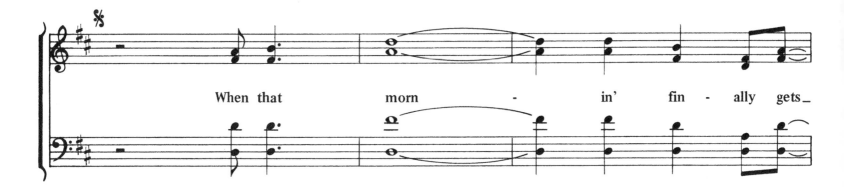

When that morn - in' fin - ally gets__

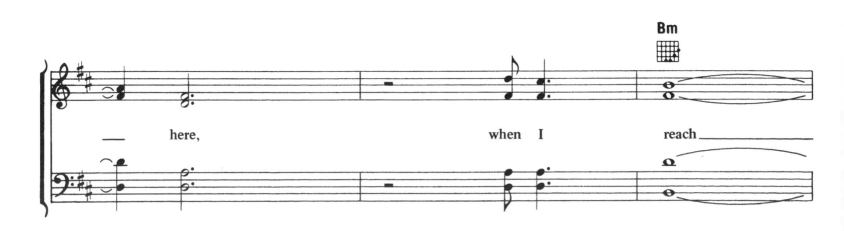

__ here, when I reach_____

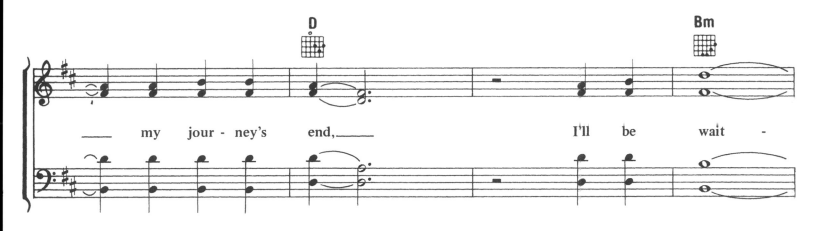

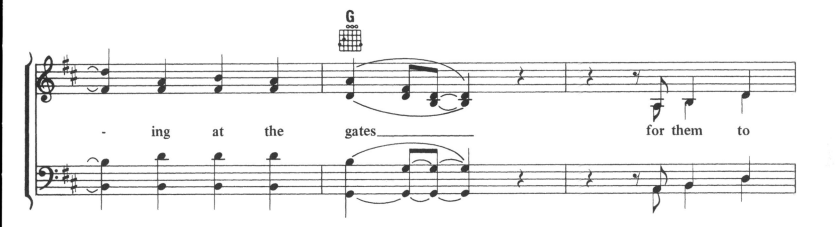

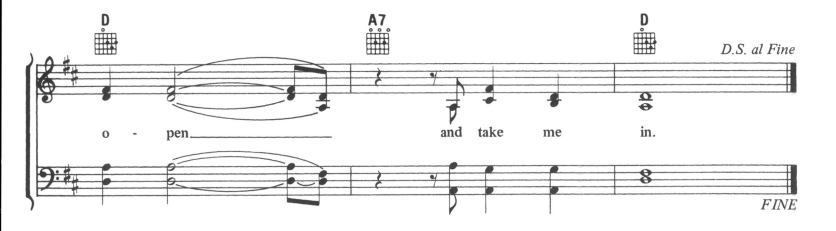

2. I have passed a lot of signs that have led me to this place;
And I know I'm on the right way;
to the day when I will see His face.

Safely In The Arms Of Jesus

By SONNY THROCKMORTON

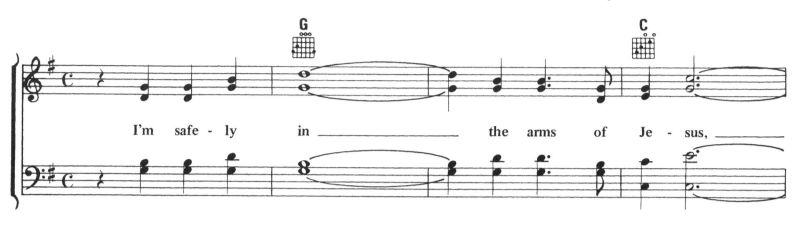

I'm safe-ly in _____ the arms of Je-sus, _____

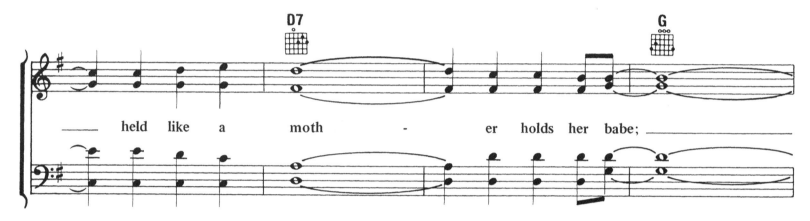

_____ held like a moth - er holds her babe; _____

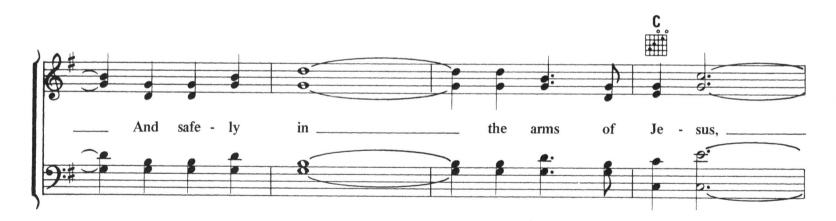

_____ And safe-ly in _____ the arms of Je-sus, _____

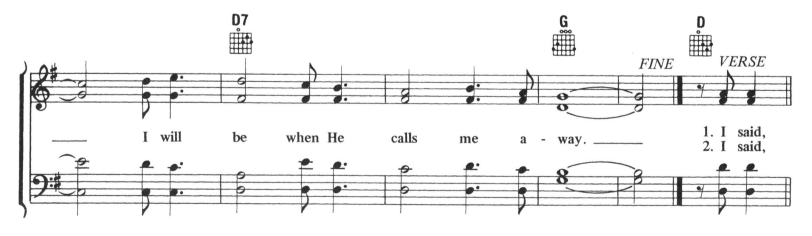

_____ I will be when He calls me a - way. _____

FINE   VERSE

1. I said,
2. I said,

"Old - time preach - er man, ___ can you help me un - der - stand ___
"Old - time preach - er man, ___ have you got a plan, ___ 'cause

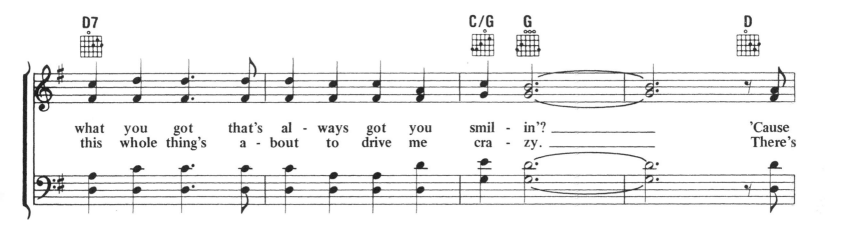

what you got that's al - ways got you smil - in'? _____ 'Cause
this whole thing's a - bout to drive me cra - zy. _____ There's

I'm a - fraid to die, and I don't know how to live." ___ He picked up ___
so man - y ways to go, and you know, I just don't know." ___ A

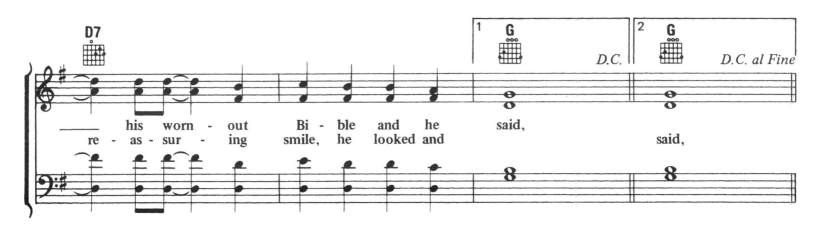

___ his worn - out Bi - ble and he said,
re - as - sur - ing smile, he looked and said,

That's The Man I'm Looking For

By DON LEE

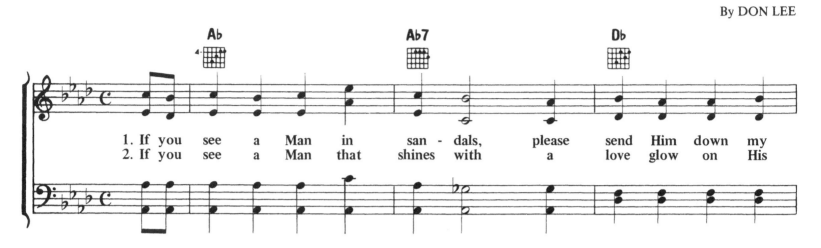

1. If you see a Man in san - dals, please send Him down my
2. If you see a Man that shines with a love glow on His

way; It might be my Mas - ter__ He's com - ing back__ some
face; Turn Him down my street_____ So He can find__ my

day; If you see a Man in white that's like no one you've seen be -
place; And__ if His hands are scarred_____ please don't shut the

fore,_____ Won't you let me know,
door, Just send Him on to me,

That's the Man I'm look - ing

for. And if you can re-mem-ber, ask Him what's His

name; And if He tells you Je-sus, say, "We're so glad You

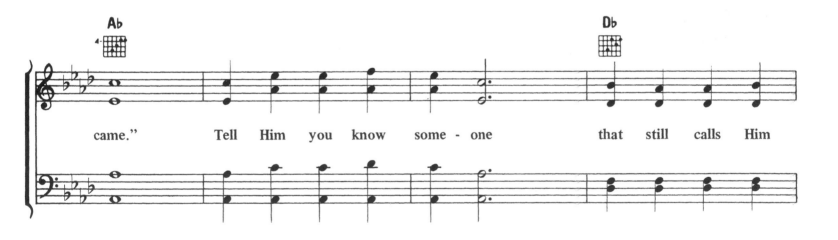

came." Tell Him you know some-one that still calls Him

Lord, Then send Him on to me, that's the Man I'm look-ing for.

Turn Your Radio On

By ALBERT E. BRUMLEY

1. Come and lis-ten in to a ra-di-o sta-tion where the might-y hosts of Heav-en sing,
2. Broth-er lis-ten in to the glo-ry land cho-rus, lis-ten to the glad ho-san-nas roll, Turn your ra-di-o
3. Lis-ten to the songs of the fa-thers and moth-ers and the man-y friends gone on be-fore,

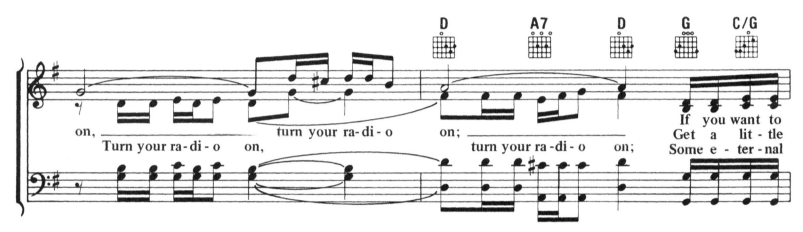

on, _____ turn your ra-di-o on; _____ If you want to
Turn your ra-di-o on, turn your ra-di-o on; Get a lit-tle
Some e-ter-nal

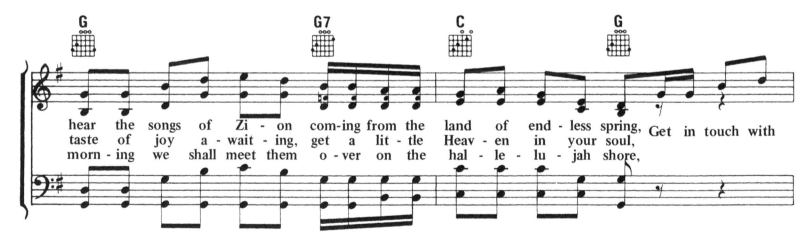

hear the songs of Zi-on com-ing from the land of end-less spring, Get in touch with
taste of joy a-wait-ing, get a lit-tle Heav-en in your soul,
morn-ing we shall meet them o-ver on the hal-le-lu-jah shore,

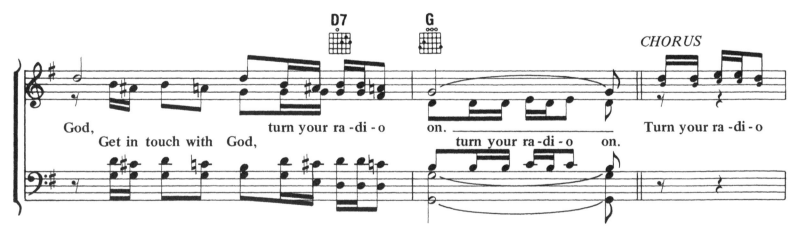

God, turn your ra-di-o on. *CHORUS*
Get in touch with God, turn your ra-di-o on. Turn your ra-di-o

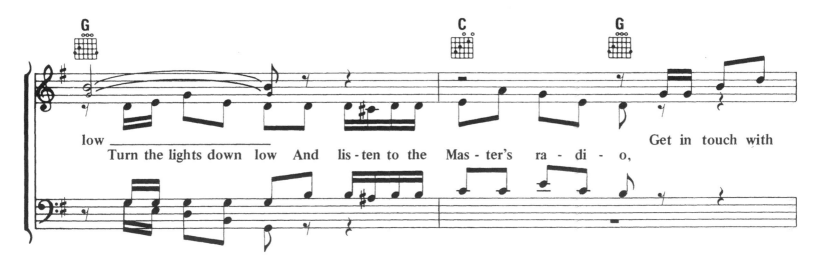

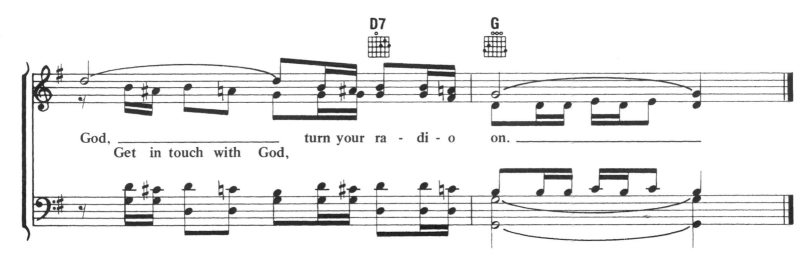

A Thing Called Love

By JERRY HUBBARD

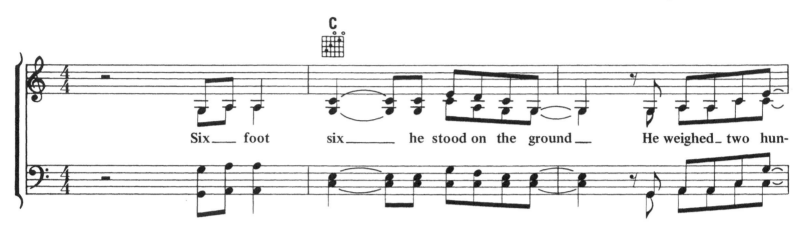

Six_ foot six___ he stood on the ground __ He weighed_ two hun-

-dred and thir - ty five pounds, But I saw__that gi - ant of a man_brought__

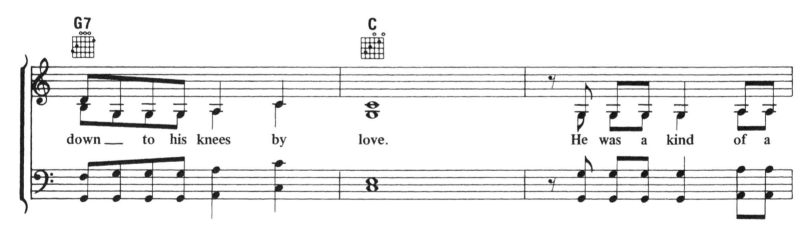

down __ to his knees by love. He was a kind of a

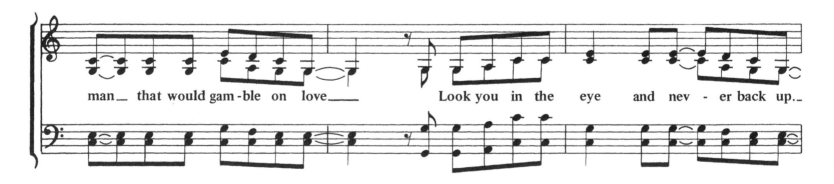

man_ that would gam-ble on love___ Look you in the eye and nev - er back up._

But I saw him cry - in' like a lit - tle whipped pup____ be - cause of

love. You can't see it with your eyes, hold it in your hand, But like the

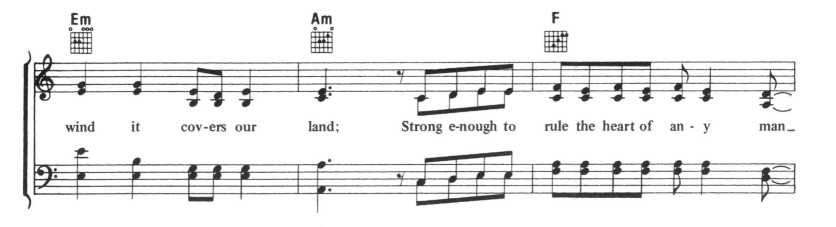

wind it cov-ers our land; Strong e-nough to rule the heart of an - y man____

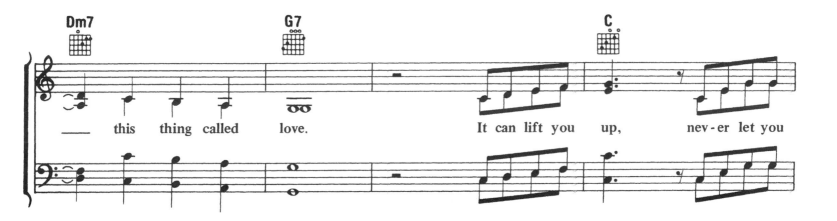

____ this thing called love. It can lift you up, nev - er let you

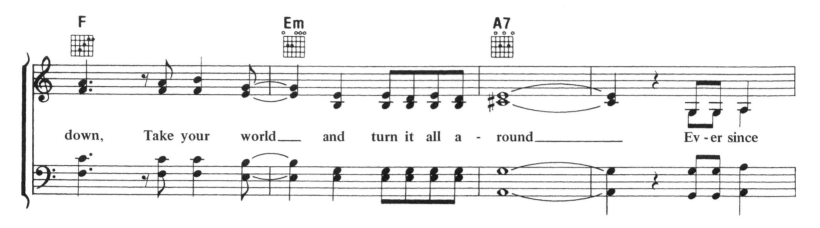

down, Take your world___ and turn it all a - round_____ Ev - er since

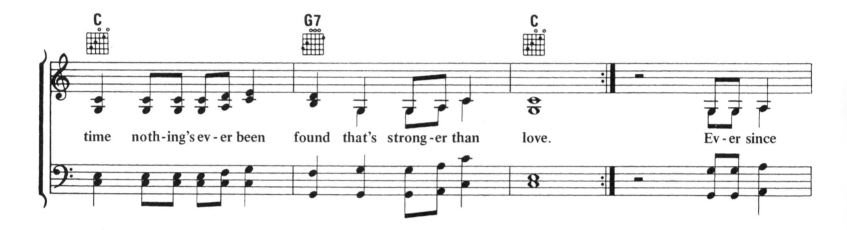

time noth-ing's ev - er been found that's strong-er than love. Ev - er since

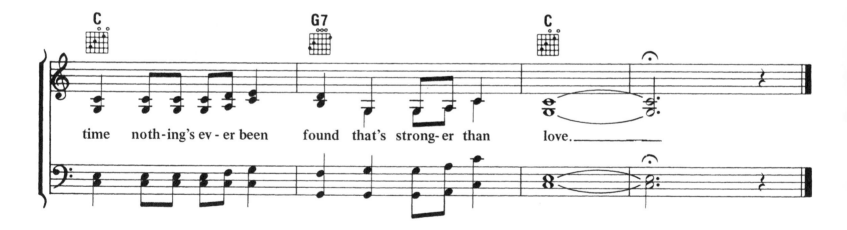

time noth-ing's ev - er been found that's strong-er than love._____

2. Most men like me struggle in doubt,
   They trouble their minds day in and day out,
   Too busy with livin' to worry a-bout a little word like love.

3. But when I see a mother's tenderness,
   As she holds her young close to her breast,
   Then I thank God that the world's been blessed
   with a thing called love.

The Unclouded Day

1. O they tell me of a home far be-yond the sky, O they tell me of a home _ far a-
2. O they tell me of a home where my friends have gone, O they tell me of a land _ far a-
3. O they tell me that He smiles on His chil-dren there, And His smile _ drives _ sor-rows all a-

way; Yes, they tell me of a home where no storms ev-er rise, O they tell me of an un-cloud-ed day.
way; O they tell me of a tree in e-ter-nal bloom, O they tell me of a love-ly _ land.
way; And they tell me that no heart-aches shall ev-er come, O that love-ly land of un-cloud-ed day.

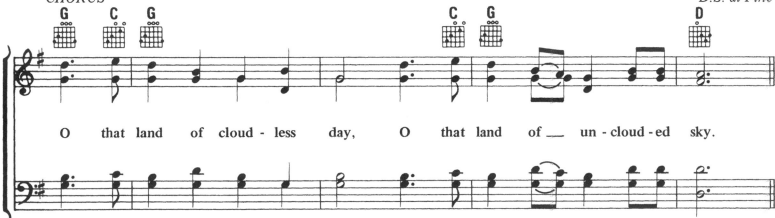

CHORUS

O that land of cloud-less day, O that land of _ un-cloud-ed sky.

The Wayfaring Stranger

1. I am a poor way-far-ing strang-er, While trav-'ling thru this world be-low; There is no
2. I want to sing Sal-va-tion's sto-ry in con-cert with the blood-washed band; I want to
3. I'll soon be free from ev-'ry tri-al, this form will rest be-neath the sod; I'll drop the

sick-ness, toil, nor dan-ger in that bright world to which I go. I'm go-ing there to meet my
wear a crown of glo-ry, when I get home to that good land. I'm go-ing there to meet the
cross of self de-ni-al, and en-ter in my home with God. I'm go-ing there to see my

Fa-ther, I'm go-ing there no more to roam;
saved ones who passed be-fore me one by one; } I am just go-ing o-ver Jor-dan, I am just go-ing o-ver home.
Sav-ior, who shed for me His pre-cious blood;

Will The Circle Be Unbroken

Words by ADA R. HABERSHON
Music by CHARLES H. GABRIEL

1. I was stand-ing by my win-dow, on one cold and cloud-y
2. Oh, I told the un-der-tak-er, "Un-der-tak-er please drive
3. I will fol-low close be-hind her, try to hold up and be

day. When I saw the hearse come roll-ing, For to take my Moth-er a-way.
slow. For this bod-y you are haul-ing, Lord, I hate to see her___ go".
brave. But I could not hide my sor-row, When they laid her in her___ grave.

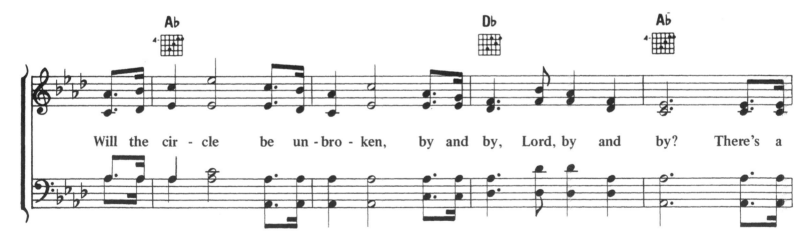

Will the cir-cle be un-bro-ken, by and by, Lord, by and by? There's a

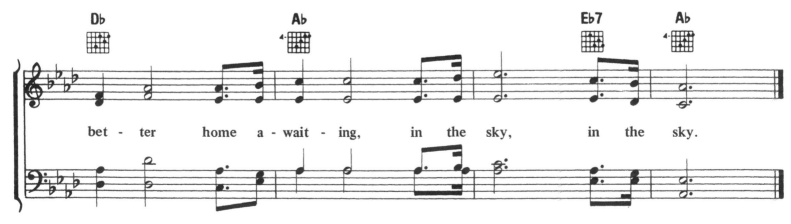

bet-ter home a-wait-ing, in the sky, in the sky.

Wings Of A Dove

By BOB FERGUSON

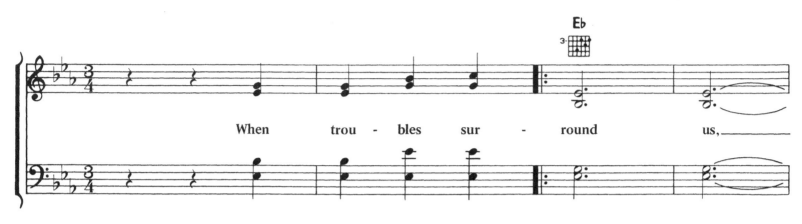

When trou - bles sur - round us,

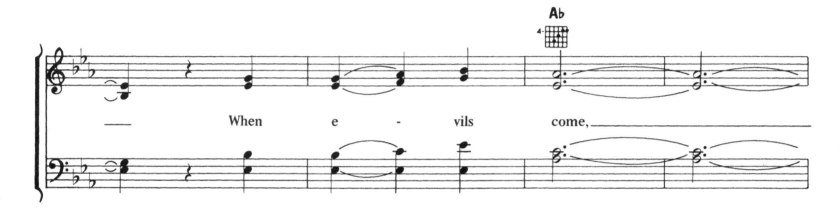

When e - vils come,

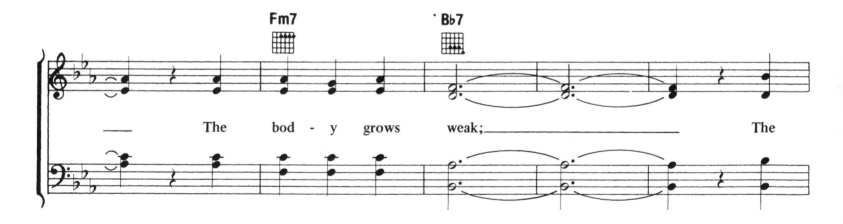

The bod - y grows weak; The

spir - it grows numb. When these things be - set The

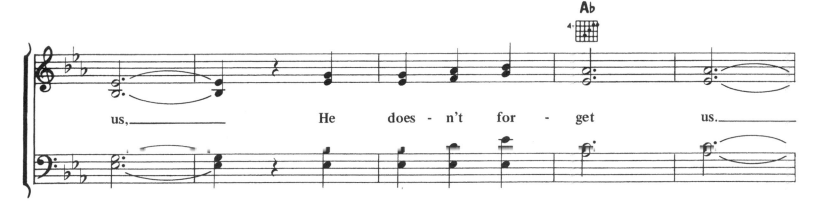

us,_____ He does - n't for - get us._____

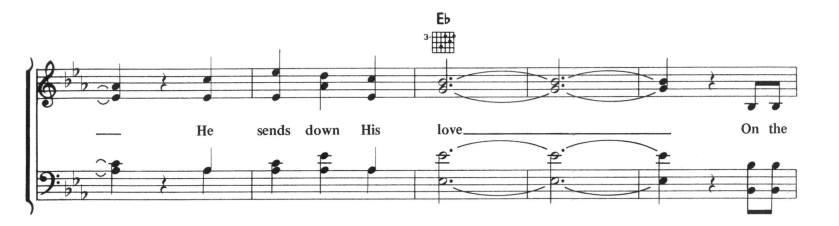

__ He sends down His love_____ On the

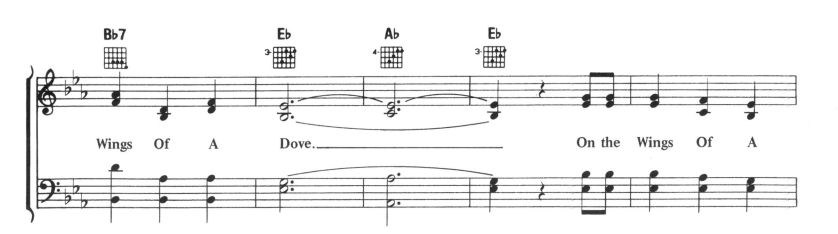

Wings Of A Dove._____ On the Wings Of A

Snow White Dove He sends His pure

sweet love, A sign from a - bove_____

_____ On The Wings Of A Dove._____ 2. When

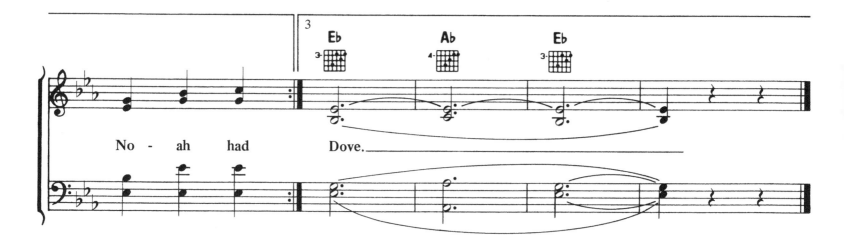

No - ah had Dove._____

2. When Noah had drifted on the flood many days,
   He searched for land in various ways.
   Troubles he had some but wasn't forgotten,
   He sent him His love On The Wings Of A Dove.

3. When Jesus went down to the waters that day,
   He was baptized in the usual way.
   When it was done, God blessed His Son.
   He sent Him His love On The Wings Of A Dove.